NORTH DEVON MOODS

PETER HENDRIE

HALSGROVE

First published in Great Britain in 2003

Copyright © 2003 Peter Hendrie
www.wild-encounters.com

Title page photograph: A walk on the wild side
*A mist descends over the dunes as this boardwalk leads you
through the nature reserve of Braunton Burrows.*

British Library Cataloguing-in-Publication Data
A CIP record for this title is available from the British Library

ISBN 1 84114 317 0

HALSGROVE
Halsgrove House
Lower Moor Way
Tiverton, Devon EX16 6SS
Tel: 01884 243242
Fax: 01884 243325
email: sales@halsgrove.com
website: www.halsgrove.com

Printed and bound
in Italy by D'Auria Industrie Grafiche Spa

INTRODUCTION

Many who visit North Devon carry away images of chocolate-box villages and the dramatic, imposing coastline. There is, however, so much more to the place than that and in these photographs I have sought to depict the true diversity of an area near to my heart.

A strong dependency on farming has helped shape much of the patchwork landscape, punctuated by mature hedgerows, and yet parts survive which are purely wild and natural, helping to make up the rich tapestry of colour which is North Devon. The rugged coastline, for example, has been shaped by the second- highest tidal fall in the world, both spectacular and hostile. Inland, undulating moorland is of a quieter, gentler, more hospitable nature, dressed in vibrant purple heather and rich golden gorse.

I have endeavoured to capture what I think is the essence of landscape, looking for the unusual or remote in a much-treasured scene. The lighting here changes in an instant – along with the weather! Much has been made of the hour preceding dusk and after dawn, for to me they conjure up a feeling of anticipation, a promise, theatrical skies or low light casting shadows which bathe the land in an ethereal glow.

My fascination with the landscape never wanes. Dressed in seasonal colours the scene changes from day to day, and capturing these moods in all their perfection is the object I strive to achieve. It might be the Atlantic Ocean crashing relentlessly over rocky outcrops of the majestic coastline or one of the many waterfalls cascading down the rocks falling back into the sea; the freshness of spring, with its plethora of green, embellishing miles and miles of beech hedges and trees; or acres of wild flowers hugging the cliff-tops and welcoming walkers, from the Cornish border in the west to the Somerset border in the east.

When looking at many of my photographs you might see one thing missing – people! I am hoping to arouse your senses, your sight, your hearing, even your sense of smell, experiencing the remoteness and the solitude, stimulating your imagination to stand in the very heart of this ever-changing scene. Because, of course, you are that missing person experiencing the glorious moment I have striven to portray.

Peter Hendrie
2003

LOCATION MAP

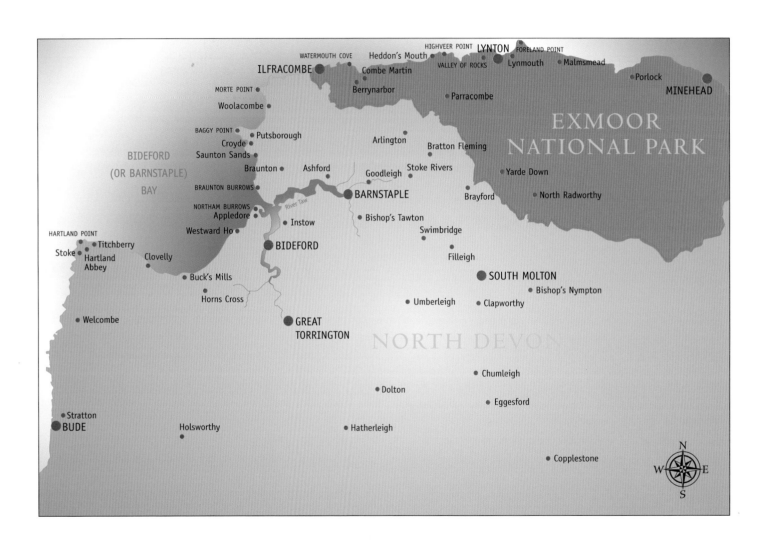

HIGHVEER POINT **LYNTON** FORELAND POINT
WATERMOUTH COVE   Heddon's Mouth
ILFRACOMBE   Combe Martin   VALLEY OF ROCKS   Lynmouth • Malmsmead
   Berrynarbor   • Porlock
MORTE POINT •   Parracombe   **MINEHEAD**
Woolacombe •   Parracombe

**EXMOOR
NATIONAL PARK**

BAGGY POINT •   Putsborough   Arlington   Bratton Fleming
   Croyde •   Bratton Fleming
BIDEFORD   Saunton Sands •   Goodleigh   Stoke Rivers   • Yarde Down
(OR BARNSTAPLE)   Braunton •   Ashford
BAY   BRAUNTON BURROWS •   Goodleigh • Stoke Rivers   Brayford   • North Radworthy
   River Taw   **BARNSTAPLE**
NORTHAM BURROWS •   • Instow   • Bishop's Tawton
   Appledore •   • Bishop's Tawton
HARTLAND POINT   Westward Ho •   Swimbridge
• Titchberry   **BIDEFORD**   Filleigh
Stoke •   Hartland   Clovelly •   **SOUTH MOLTON**
Abbey   • Buck's Mills   • Bishop's Nympton
   • Horns Cross   • Umberleigh   • Clapworthy
• Welcombe   **GREAT
TORRINGTON**   **NORTH DEVON**
   • Chumleigh
   • Dolton
   • Eggesford
• Stratton
BUDE   Holsworthy   • Hatherleigh
   • Copplestone

N
W   E
S

Gushing
*Watersmeet after a deluge
of rain, sees the river quicken as it
cascades down to Lynmouth.*

Pot of purple and gold
Viewed from Great Hangman just as a storm passes over.

Woodland glade
Molland plantation near Brayford takes on an atmospheric air when shrouded in an early-morning autumn mist.

Peeping through
*Foreland Point drives a dividing line between a celestial sky and its reflected
light on the water beneath. Shot from Hurlstone Point on the coast fringe of Somerset.*

Sugar coated (just a reminder)
A light dusting of snow provides a gentle reminder of winter.
Shot from Five Burrows Hill a candy-coloured sky reflects warm hues on the snow.

Singled out

The florid colour and mottled texture of a pebble, starkly contrasted with the soft hues and tones of its surroundings, demand attention.

Cove at Hartland

The curvature of the coastline provides a perfect frame for the linear scars driven into the rock over thousands of years.

Little Hangman
*A bold line of heather in the foreground
is punctuated by a single cluster of
vibrant yellow gorse, with the crest
of Little Hangman forming a perfect
break to the lofty ridge.*

Toadstools on nursing stump
*A moist winter's morning adds an intensity of colour to an ancient stump,
which supports a rich array of epiphytic mosses and lichens topped by
caramel-coloured toadstools, in woodland near Brendon.*

Theatrical skies
Like the closing scene of an epic play, pulling together all the main elements of the plot in one final spectacle.
(The inclusion of this picture as my personal favourite smudges the county borders of Exmoor).

Ingrained
An intimate look at the majestic lines of age, give this piece of wood depth and beauty. Turned one way 'the nose of a bear', another 'a slender-necked maiden.'

Watercourse

The turbulent unrestrained passage of water, as it spills down rocks near Rockford.

Babbacombe Cliff
*Vibrant russet tones of the cliff line of Babbacombe, radiating the last rays of sunlight in the early evening,
the polished pebbles at the water-line a resplendent, gunmetal grey.*

Hartland Point lighthouse
*The natural play of light and shade
bring a luminescent quality to the
lighthouse and add a sense of foreboding
to the seascape, with Lundy Island
sitting defiantly in the background.*

Rounded

A pebble sits resolute, as water gushes relentlessly about it, its rounded form a product of torrential cascading waters. Shot at Lynmouth.

Tapestry

I love the mix of structure and interlocking forms in this photograph taken at West Tichberry Farm. The angular lines and block colours of cultivated fields reaching into the distance, are in sharp contrast to the irregularity and disorder of nature in the foreground.

Ethereal glow

Peppercombe near Horns Cross, bathed in last light on a tranquil evening in May. The pebble ridge is seemingly positioned to face the sun, like a sun seeker catching the last rays.

Burrow land
Lobb Hill.

Mud-flats
*Positioned like intricate pieces of a jigsaw puzzle these mud-flats
overlook the village of Appledore, famous for its shipbuilding. The rosy
pink hue brings warmth to a cold January evening.*

Flats Pill
*One of the many tiny waterways that help to make up the
Biosphere Reserve of Braunton Marsh.*

Singled out
Taken at the Taw-Torridge estuary near Yell Pool,
laid to rest temporarily by the tide.

Snowdrops
A multitude of snowdrops carpeting Holewater near Brayford.

Opposite: Amber light
*The ebony silhouette of Braunton Burrows serves as a foil to
a lavish amber and honey-coloured sky.*

Triumphal arch
Part of the Castle Hill Estate at Filleigh, this Grade 1 listed landmark is perfectly edged by the tree line.

Opposite: Sculpture
Like the decaying frames of an old vessel protruding from beneath the sand, these timbers bathed in soft-hued light, add to a rich feel of colour and texture.

Castle Hill

Home to the Fortescue family, Castle Hill is a unique eighteenth-century house set in 5000 acres of truly magnificent parkland.

Icicles
*Suspended like daggers from the top
of this siding near Yarde Down.*

Frozen in time
*A perfectly frozen bramble,
temporarily preserved
in the depths of winter.*

Still falls
*After days of sub-zero
temperatures in January, this
small fall near Yarde Down is
brought to a standstill.*

Woodland glade
A multitude of bluebells covers acres of land at Chenson Farm, Chenson, in a profusion of blue.

Blue versus green
Fighting for domination of woodland at Chenson Farm. A sapphire carpet of bluebells contrasts with the viridity of these fresh young beech leaves.

Overgrown
*A fresh growth of brambles
overruns this patch of bugle in
woodland near Bishop's Nympton.*

Return journey

*After days of heavy rainfall, converging brooks tumble their contents over falls at Welcombe
Mouth on their journey back to the beginning of the cycle in the Atlantic Ocean.*

Shipwrecked
Beached and broken, decaying with rust, a wreck near Hartland Point takes a relentless pounding from the surge of the Atlantic.

Funnel of trees
*The single tree to the left of centre appears as though it has been excluded
from the beech and oak coppice wood near Bishop's Nympton.*

Two moors apart
With Dartmoor in the distance seemingly deprived of snow, the landscape is partitioned
by the patchwork of fields and hedgerows which typifies Devon. Exmoor in the
foreground is animated by a dusting of snow, at Kinsford Cross.

Atlantic swell
White-crested waves pound the coastline off of Morte Point. The vivid turquoise sea is given depth by the cloudy sullen May sky.

Wintry sway

After the passing of a snowstorm, these beech trees take on a surreal quality,
with their trunks and branches covered in a veil of snow.

Opposite: Fields of amber

Ablaze in a flame-coloured glow, the last rays of light ignite Radworthy and beyond.

Up and over
Lines of hedges, following the contours of the land, rising towards Malmsmead Hill
with a lone hawthorn tree standing guard at the bottom.

Singled out
Highlighted in early-morning light, azure bluebells embellish
a woodland floor of wild garlic near Hartland.

Canopy of green
Stems of giant gunnera manicata *are protected by armour of tiny spikes,*
the image shrouded in a canopy of green.

Georgian interior
The largely eighteenth-century furnishings of St Petrock's church, Parracombe.

Long Stone
*Exmoor's tallest single standing
stone, Long Stone stands near
Chapman Barrows. Dating has been
estimated to somewhere between the late
Neolithic and early Bronze Age.
The solitary slate stone stands at
3 metres, like a finger pointing skywards.*

Spring into life
*An abundance of daffodils gilds the
woodland floor at Six Acre Wood near
Lee Bay. A pleasant reminder of spring.*

Weathered

*A temporary reprieve from the elements, as these pebbles soak up the afternoon sun before
being engulfed once more by the Atlantic, on Zulu Bank near Appledore.*

Withered blackthorn
A lone survivor, twisted and gnarled by the excesses of strong winds from the Atlantic, whipping across Exmoor.

Drawing-up
Viewed from Fyldon Common, a high viewpoint overlooking much of North Devon, sinister-looking clouds roll in from the Atlantic.

Valley of Rocks
Barren, often bleak, this piece of
coastline has an almost mystical
quality – the Valley of Rocks,
running through Woody Bay and
on to Highveer Point.

Reaching out

The branches of the trees, growing from the right-hand side of their
trunks, reach out for the available light in this thickly
covered coppice at Myrtleberry Cleave near Watersmeet.

Mythical land

Imaginations run wild, whilst sitting in Chapman Barrows, in awe-inspiring light like this.
They are thought to be ancient burial sites dating back to around the Bronze Age. Thomas
Westcote in 1630 wrote, 'Fiery dragons have been seen flying and lighting on them.'
The dragon in the sky was certainly on fire that evening.

Opposite: Gauter Point

The smooth rounded boulders in the foreground have the look and tactile quality of
velvet when set against the more rugged rocks of Gauter Point.

Forging through
Fresh water cascades down the cliff face at Buck's Mills, disappearing beneath the pebbles, re-emerging beside the large boulders and working its way back to the sea.

Blackchurch Rock
Twilight overlooking Clovelly and Blackchurch Rock, tones in the sky reflected on to the sea and rocks beneath.

Looking up to Wind Hill

The single tree at the top of Wind Hill looks like it has been plucked from
the coppice wood. It also lends a sense of scale to the picture.

Isolated barn
*Peeping through the reeds on Horsey Island this run-down
barn is one of many dotted throughout the island.*

Dusk at Watermouth
On this rare occasion with the Atlantic Ocean like a mill pond, an eerie light falls over Watermouth Cove with Little and Great Hangman, Highveer Point and Foreland Point lighthouse in the distance.

Dunes
*Braunton Burrows form the largest such
area in Britain, and are a haven for wildlife.*

Opposite: A walk on the wild side
*A mist descends over the dunes as this boardwalk leads you
through the nature reserve of Braunton Burrows.*

Mirror image
The reflection of Castle Hill in the estate's lake accentuates the intensity of the impending storm.

Reeds
The colour of the sunlit reeds dominates the Torridge river bank near Dolton.

Woven together
Entwined shades of green.

Last post
Groynes at Crow Point silhouetted against the evening sky.

Rock layers
Compressed over thousands of years, an exposed rock face at Welcombe Mouth.
The pebbles in the foreground give a sense of scale.

Opposite: High and dry
An old fishing vessel beached on mud and sand flats near Crow Point
off the Taw estuary lies in a ruinous state.

Boundary line
What was once part of the Royal Forest of Exmoor lies to the right of this boundary line running on past Chapman Barrows.

Threatening skies
Under brooding clouds the strand of the Taw at Barnstaple is tinged with a hint of mauve.

Wintry haze
Sheep graze peacefully in a field at Churchtown near Brendon.

Leading line
Fascinating rock formations at Welcombe Mouth.

Instow at sunset
A warm winter's evening sun spotlights the houses along the waterfront at Instow. Shot from Braunton Burrows.

Packhorse bridge
*Only a few of these ancient bridges remain in the area. This one at
Challacombe is a gentle reminder of a bygone age.*

Golden glow
Ever-changing light can transform even the dullest evening with a golden glow, reflected here in the freshwater stream wending its way back to the sea.

A sense of scale
Two stone barns, one slate roofed the other thatched, one rectangular the other round.
A tight perspective gives a sense of scale to this shot from Braunton Marsh.

Sunset over Heddon's Mouth
*The sun, a golden orb, settles on
the horizon, creating a dramatic
silhouette of the coastline.*

Meadowsweet
These cuckoo flowers (lady's smock) drift around in the breeze in a meadow at
Hartland Abbey, giving a sweet aroma of spring in the air.

Carpet of primrose
Slopes of a woodland glade at Stoke patterned with a profusion of primroses.

Flat calm

A real sense of calm, with only the water around the rocks in the foreground showing some sense of motion in an otherwise calm sea, at Putsborough overlooking Woolacombe Bay.

Heddon's Mouth
A snaking brook wends its way through a steep-sided combe to Highveer Rocks
and Heddon's Beach, illuminated by the sun's last rays.

Leading the way

Like an army tramping into battle these beech hedges, a feature of Exmoor,
intersect the land, creating a patchwork of irregular shapes
and sizes as they march from combe to combe.

St Paul's Church, Filleigh
*I particularly like the construction of the church with its rounded gable end
and red-tiled roof caught in mid-morning winter's light.*

Opposite: Sky of fire
*Looking down on Shortacombe towards North Radworthy, the sky ablaze with colour,
rays of light picking out the River Mole in the middle distance.*

Complementary
The pretty village of Croyde,
illuminated in the late-afternoon light,
with its white-painted houses in
the left foreground, complements
Woolacombe in the distance.

Point of interest
Like a hand reaching out to touch Lundy in the distance, this flower-clad point at Barley Bay near Hartland basks in spring sunshine.

Miniature landscape
Often missed, always there. When next out walking, stop, look down
and you will be amazed at what can be seen underfoot.

Profusion of garlic
When I got home everyone was avoiding me like the plague, I wonder why?
A riot of wild garlic stretching over acres and acres like no other I have seen. The smell was
amazing in this secret wood near Berrynarbor.

Lee Abbey

Looking out over Lee Abbey and Duty Point Tower from Crock Point, gives a feeling of serenity and stillness in the fading light.

Holwell Castle motte and bailey
The motte and earthworks are all that remain of the eleventh-century hilltop castle near Parracombe.

First light
As the sun rises on the horizon, this scene of Clovelly is painted with a warm rich glow.

Silver mines
*One of the few remnants of mining left in this area. The tower of a disused silver mine near
Combe Martin has become a much-loved landmark.*

Taking a pounding
*Waves crashing over rocks at
Barricane Beach, Woolacombe.
The force of the waves often
yields up treasures on to this rock
stretch of Woolacombe.*

From Devon with love
*This thatched cottage is the quintessential image of Devon that many
visitors carry home with them. No.2 Mill Cottage, Arlington.*

Opposite: Eldern Point
*Eldern Point near Titchberry stands out against a long
cast shadow, and cheery yellow gorse.*

Springtime at Hartland Abbey

Red campion spills over the verge on the left of the fence, with young oak leaves beginning to appear and
bullocks grazing in a meadow filled with cuckoo flowers and buttercups: spring is truly upon us.

Devon framework

A true perception of rural North Devon: elegant farmhouses, run-down barns with rusting roofs, a maze of tiny lanes and tracks threading through the countryside; fields framed by miles and miles of hedgerows and trees; a colourful tapestry as the fields change from season to season. Who in their right mind would want to live anywhere else?

Threatening to erupt
Sinister-looking clouds about to erupt over Bideford (or Barnstaple) Bay with Hartland Point in the distance.

Painted hill
Like a beacon sending out a flash of light, Codden Hill is crested in vibrant yellow.
On closer inspection you can see a shade of yellow in almost everything,
as the warmth from the low, setting sun has created just that.

Sea of yellow
The path leads from right to left, until you reach the wooden fence, creating a desire to discover what lies around the corner. Codden Hill near Barnstaple, animated by the swaying crop of rapeseed.

Shining oak
Like the principal actor on the stage, this backlit oak
glistens in the limelight of spring.

Opposite: Trickling down
This trickling brook at Badgworthy Water in Lorna Doone
country carries with it remnants of autumn.

Soft illumination
A warm glow descends over Lee Bay with Lee Abbey in the distance, from Crock Point.

Primrose bank
Morning glory, as these primroses enjoy the best of the morning sunlight in woodland near Hartland Abbey.

Shades of green
*Strong side-lighting on an overcast day illuminates selected trees in Molland
Wood near Brayford, placing an emphasis on shape and colour.*

Isolated church
This isolated church at Brendon is well over a mile from its village. It draws its
congregation from miles around, like many rural churches.

Sea Pinks
*The cliff face covered with thrift at
Blegberry Beach near Hartland Quay,
maintaining its colour in the face of all
that the elements can throw at it.*

Brendon

The tiny village of Brendon is situated in the northwest of Exmoor on the banks of the East Lyn river.

Where two rivers meet
Farley Water joins Hoaroak Water upstream before surging down waterfalls and merging with the East Lyn river at Watersmeet.

Sea flowers
*A collage of sea flowers, thrift, kidney vetch and common scurvy grass, to name
but a few, help to make up this picturesque bank at Blegberry Beach.*

Fisherman's cottage
*Early-morning light illuminates
this fisherman's cottage perched
on the edge of Clovelly.
There is anticipation of
a good drying day.*

High and dry
Just as the tide recedes, reflections from the boats appear in the wet muddy sand of Lynmouth harbour.

Long shadows
*Long shadows cast by the low sun
help to create depth in this pretty
cobbled street in Clovelly.*

Sea Mist

The coastline around Lynmouth and the Valley of Rocks, often seen shrouded in sea mist. The early-morning sun tries to burn the mist to reveal Duty Point and Highveer Point in the distance.

Parallel lines
These lines of turned grass, drying in the late-afternoon sun near Clapworthy Mill,
add a sense of conformity to an otherwise unmanaged rural landscape.

Lobster pots
*Lobster pots lined up on Clovelly quay waiting to go back out to sea,
a long-standing tradition with local fisherman.*

Buttercup meadow
*Two parallel lines, the river and the fence, lead you through the scene
to the island in the middle distance on the River Mole.*

Early purple orchids
*Found in hedgerows, woodland, coppices and scrub throughout North Devon,
these perennial plants flower between April to June with vibrant purple
flowers in rich contrast to the vibrant green grasses of the bank.*

Opposite: Reflections
*Two clinker-built fishing boats, not dissimilar to those formerly built at Appledore,
which has a fine tradition in boat and ship construction. Reflections in
the waters of the Inner Pool at Clovelly.*

Devon longhouse
*Spectacular in construction, Crosse Farm near Bishop's Nympton is a fine
example of a Devon longhouse and exudes character and charm.*

Pastures green
Sheep and cattle graze in lush green pastures surrounded by ancient oak and beech trees at Barnacott Farm.

Disappearing road
Viewed from Oxen Tor the distant road disappears under a canopy of trees as it runs through Glen Lyn Gorge towards Watersmeet.

Broccoli?

*Looking down over Hester Wood in subdued light this canopy of trees looked to
me like giant broccoli stalks, as this compressed image shows.*

Majestic falls
Farley and Hoaroak Waters
join forces at Hillsford Bridge
before descending these fast-
flowing falls at Watersmeet.

Harbourside
Early morning, at Clovelly, before the bustle of the day gives life to the sleepy harbour.

Moored up
*A line of fishing boats moored up
alongside the harbour at Clovelly.*

Just lit
A stark reminder to shipping of treacherous coastline.

Opposite: Jetting out
Dusk falls over this famous coastal fishing village – Clovelly.

Transmission of light
*A stunning mix of light and shade, as the last light of day creates a dramatic lighting effect,
with the clouds adding a key feature to this shot of Holdstone Down.*

Heavenly glow
Crimson skies reflect a sense of quiescence on this scene, a feeling of warmth radiates even on this cool spring evening.